SCHOLASTIC
News
Nonfiction Readers

A Ladybug Larva Grows Up

by Katie Marsico

Children's Press
An Imprint of Scholastic Inc.
New York Toronto London Auckland Sydney
Mexico City New Delhi Hong Kong
Danbury, Connecticut

These content vocabulary word builders are for grades 1–2.

Subject Consultant: Susan H. Gray, MS, Zoology

Reading Consultant: Cecilia Minden-Cupp, PhD, Former Director of the Language and Literacy Program, Harvard Graduate School of Education, Cambridge, Massachusetts

Photographs © 2007: Bruce Coleman Inc./John Shaw: 23 top right; Dembinsky Photo Assoc.: 5 top left,11, 20 bottom (Anthony Mercieca), 4 bottom left, 6, 23 bottom right (Gary Meszaros); Dwight R. Kuhn Photography: cover left inset, cover center inset, 2 top, 4 bottom right, 5 bottom left, 5 top right, 7, 10, 13, 17, 20 right, 20 center left, 21 bottom, 21 top, 23 bottom left; Getty Images/Digital Vision: cover right inset, 9, 20 top left; NHPA/Stephen Dalton: cover background; Photo Researchers, NY: back cover, 5 bottom right, 15, 19, 21 center (Nature's Images), 23 top left (Perennou Nuridsany), 1, 4 top, 16 (Harry Rogers).

Book Design: Simonsays Design!
Book Production: The Design Lab

Library of Congress Cataloging-in-Publication Data
Marsico, Katie, 1980–
    A ladybug larva grows up / By Katie Marsico.
       p. cm. — (Scholastic news nonfiction readers)
    Includes bibliographical references and index.
    ISBN-13: 978-0-531-17478-4 (lib. bdg)   978-0-531-18697-8 (pbk.)
    ISBN-10: 0-531-17478-6 (lib. bdg)   0-531-18697-0 (pbk.)
    1. Ladybugs—Development—Juvenile literature. I. Title. II. Series.
    QL596.C65M28 2007
    595.76'9—dc22   2006025609

2 3 4 5 6 7 8 9 10 R 17 16 15 14 13 12 11 10 09

CONTENTS

WORD HUNT

Look for these words as you read. They will be in **bold**.

adult
(**ah**-duhlt)

insects
(**in**-sekts)

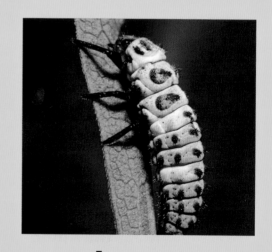

larva
(**lar**-vuh)

4

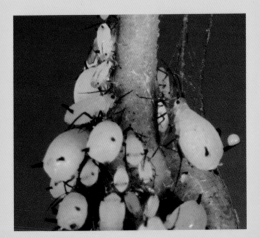

aphids
(**ay**-fidz)

hatching
(**hach**-ing)

molting
(**molt**-ing)

pupa
(**pyoo**-puh)

Ladybug Larvae

What is a ladybug **larva**?

A larva is a baby ladybug.

Ladybugs are **insects**. Insects have six legs and two feelers. Many insects have wings.

insect

All baby insects are called larvae.

First, a mother ladybug lays her eggs.

She usually lays them on the bottom side of a leaf.

The yellow eggs are sticky. This holds them in place on the leaf.

A mother ladybug lays hundreds of eggs.

After about five days, the eggs on the leaf begin **hatching**. Out come the larvae!

A ladybug larva has six legs and no wings.

The babies are hungry. They soon begin eating tiny insects called **aphids**.

hatching ladybug larva

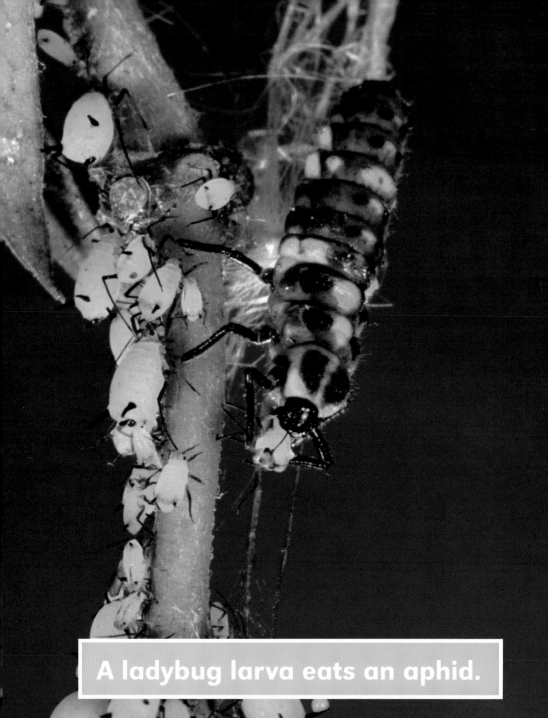

A ladybug larva eats an aphid.

The ladybug babies begin to shed their skin as they grow. This is called **molting**.

After about ten to fourteen days, a larva attaches to a plant or twig. It stays very still.

A ladybug larva usually molts three or four times.

Suddenly, the larva's skin seems to split open! Out comes a ladybug **pupa**!

A ladybug pupa has a hard shell and does not move much.

The ladybug is getting closer and closer to being a grown-up.

A ladybug pupa attaches itself to a plant to finish growing.

What's going on inside a pupa's shell? The ladybug is changing.

It is beginning to look less like a larva and more like an **adult**.

After about five days, a pupa's shell splits open. Out comes an adult ladybug!

adult

An adult ladybug comes out of its pupa shell.

You can't see the ladybug's spots at first. They become clearer over time.

Soon, the new adults will lay eggs of their own!

Different kinds of ladybugs have different numbers of spots.

A LADYBUG LARVA GROWS UP!

1

A mother ladybug lays her eggs on the bottom of a leaf.

2

The ladybug larvae hatch from their eggs in about five days.

3

The larvae are hungry! They gobble up aphids on the leaf.

6 In about five days, a pupa's shell splits. The ladybug is all grown up!

5 After about ten to fourteen days, a larva splits its skin. Out comes a pupa!

4 A ladybug larva molts, or sheds its skin, three to four times.

YOUR NEW WORDS

adult (**ah**-duhlt) a grown-up person or animal

aphids (**ay**-fidz) small insects with soft bodies that eat plant juices

hatching (**hach**-ing) breaking out of an egg

insects (**in**-sekts) small animals with six legs, two feelers, three separate body sections, and a hard shell

larva (**lar**-vuh) a baby insect, such as a ladybug, that has just hatched from its egg; two or more babies are called larvae

molting (**molt**-ing) shedding skin

pupa (**pyoo**-puh) an insect, such as a ladybug, that is no longer a larva but is not yet an adult

THESE ANIMALS ARE INSECTS, TOO!

bee

butterfly

cricket

dragonfly

INDEX

FIND OUT MORE

Book:

Finn, Isobel, and Jack Tickle (illustrator). *The Very Lazy Ladybug.* Wilton, CT: Tiger Tales, 2001.

Website:

The Ladybug Lady
http://www.ladybuglady.com/

MEET THE AUTHOR

Katie Marsico lives with her family outside of Chicago, Illinois. She doesn't mind ladybugs and often finds that they enjoy visiting her home during warmer weather.